Get Out Of Your Head
And Into Your Life!

TAKE ACTION

Don't just dream it,
Live It!

Kim Ladjevich

Get Out of Your Head and Into Your Life!
Don't just Dream it, Live It!

Kim Ladjevich

Copyright © 2015 by Kim Ladjevich
All rights reserved.

No part of this publication may be reproduced, stored in a retrieval system, transmitted in any form or by any means, electronic, mechanical, photocopying, recording, or otherwise, without prior written permission of the publisher and author/illustrator.

Designed by: Parry Design Studio, Inc. *www.parrydesign.com*

ISBN: 978-0-9962406-0-4

Printed in the U.S.A.

Dedication

To my mom and dad who always made me feel like I could do
or be anything I wanted. Thanks for always believing in me.
To my wonderful husband and amazing boys who
challenge, inspire and love me every day.
To all of you who share yourselves and your amazing
talents to make the world a better place.
I love you all.

Contents

Acknowledgments vii

Introduction xi

Cultivate the Right Attitude 1

Utilize a Great Listener. 7

Journal Your New and Good 11

Shift the Focus of Your Thoughts 15

Find Your Passion 23

Pursue Your Goals with Child-Like Persistence 29

Use Your Talents to Help Others 41

Create Affirmations 47

Understand the Power of Prayer, Meditation and Visualization 51

You Deserve This So No More Excuses 55

Thoughts for Getting Unstuck 61

Live in the Flow and Experience Synchronicity 65

Develop Consistent Habits 69

About the Author 73

Acknowledgments

First and foremost, I thank God for everything. God is the reason for my successes and the reason I have made it through the challenging times in my life. I am incredibly blessed and pray that I continue to use my talents in larger ways to help more people while giving honor and glory to God.

Secondly, I want to thank my husband Rick and boys, Ricky and Ryan for their patience and support in my writing this book. Also for all the wonderful things they've taught me. Special thanks to my brother Kevin who read my book and provided feedback for every chapter. Thank you to my parents, Fran and Jan for giving me an amazing foundation in my upbringing and most importantly my faith which is a blessing in good times and in bad.

It was faith that helped me make the decision to attend The Institute of Integrative Nutrition. (*www.integrativenutrition.com*) I believe the school and founder Joshua Rosenthal were the catalyst for moving me out of my head into my life. Attending the school inspired me like never before. The school gave me all the tools and support I needed to make big changes in my life. Because of the school and the world it opened up for me, my whole life changed and continues to evolve for the better. I am forever grateful to Joshua and the school.

I would also like to thank Joshua Rosenthal a second time and Lindsey Smith for their book writing class that provided me with the framework, motivation and tools to finish this book. Special thanks to Suzanne Boothby, my editor who worked on the first draft of this book with me. Her book coaching was invaluable. Also, thanks to Jeannine Norris who did my final editing. Thank you to Jack Parry with Parry Design Studio who did the book design and brought my vision for the cover to life.

There are too many great authors, poets, healers, inspirational speakers, family and friends, priests, teachers, coaches etc. that have influenced me to name here however, I would be remiss if I didn't mention that I have found Oprah Winfrey both personally and through her shows to be an amazing source of inspiration along with so many of the people she has had on her shows including one of my favorites the late, Maya Angelou.

Introduction

Take a moment and reflect on how quickly the last 10 years have passed and just consider how quickly the next 10 could go. Imagine laying on your deathbed and thinking how silly and insignificant the fears and excuses that kept you from pursuing your dreams will seem at that moment.

Think about your life now. Do you have amazing ideas but never share them or act upon them? Do you want a different career, a vacation home, or a new car? Maybe you would like to dance, snow ski, climb a mountain, go to college, write a book, be an artist, perform in a play, ride a horse, visit another country, be a stay-at-home mom, swim with dolphins, or ride in a helicopter.

What does your dream life look like?

Are you living it or is your life stuck on autopilot going down the wrong road?

If your life does not look the way you want it to look or you're not checking off your list of what you want to accomplish, acquire, or become, then this book is for you. Decide today to take the wheel and change direction.

I want to inspire you to take action, to stop daydreaming and start living your dreams. If you don't plan and take action to be the person you want to be and have the life you want, life will just happen. Each day will come and go, and then in a blink of an eye, years will come and go. Think about the person you want to be and your dream life. If you don't see much of it in your current reality, it's time for change.

One definition of insanity is doing the same thing over and over and expecting different results. Make up your mind today to figure out what you've been doing over and over without the results you want. Decide today to do it differently because it's not working. Put yourself in the driver's seat. It's never too late to start creating the life you want for yourself and being the person you aspire to be.

What are you waiting for?

No one is going to hand you your dream life. You have to create it. First, make up your mind that you deserve it. Then take control of your own destiny and begin today. The concepts in this book will help you in your journey.

In this book, I will share my journey—the steps I took to get out of my own head so I could begin creating my dream life. I hope it will help and support you to have your dream life too.

■

"The future is not something to where we are going to, but rather a place we are creating. The paths to it are not found; they are made."

–Jane Garvey

"All our dreams can come true if we have the courage to pursue them."

–Walt Disney

"There are some people who live in a dream world, and there are some who face reality; and then there are those who turn one into the other."

–*Desiderius Erasmus, The Best of Success*

Introduction

My own journey to getting out of my head and into my life, began when I made the decision to attend the Institute for Integrative Nutrition in New York City, the largest nutrition school in the world. This was the first big step I took towards becoming more of the person I wanted to be. I usually ignored my intuition, my gut feeling, because it often required me to get out of my comfort zone, that safe place in my head that stored all my other great thoughts and ideas. This time I took a leap of faith and didn't ignore it. Listening to my own intuition and attending this school were the best decisions I could have ever made.

Very early on in my classes, the founder and primary teacher, Joshua Rosenthal, posed this question to the students, "At lunch today, please discuss what has been holding you back from moving forward and accomplishing what you want." So I went to lunch with another student and discussed with her my lifelong problem of being stuck in my head and never taking action. What I took from our discussion was this:

Generally speaking you will always have moments when you tell yourself negative things. Don't listen to those thoughts. When you start hearing the negative voices in your head, get out of your head. Bring yourself back to the present, the here and now. Feel your breath, your heartbeat, your toes. Take yourself out of your head, away from those negative thoughts.

Our discussion offered me a way to put my racing mind to rest for a while. For years I've dealt with these negative voices and needed a way to shut them up so I could accomplish something. I'm sure anyone who has not achieved the things they want in life or who has not even tried can relate to the negative voices.

When we returned from lunch Joshua asked for someone to share what was holding them back. Inspired from my discussion at lunch, I raised my hand. He called on someone else. Thank goodness because my heart was racing and my thoughts were racing even faster! I could never have communicated anything meaningful in that state. While the person spoke, I told myself to breathe and get out of my head. I focused on what was going on in my body so that I could speak from my heart. By concentrating on my heartbeat, breathe, etc., I didn't even realize but the voices in my head stopped and I began to calm down. He then asked for another volunteer. I raised my hand and by the time Joshua called on me a complete calm had come over me. I had shifted all my thoughts to my breathing (well except for my left leg which seemed to quiver the entire time despite the calm I felt otherwise). I took the microphone, speaking to about a thousand people. I had always wanted to speak in front of a large group but had only dreamed about it in my head.

After I shared with the crowd, Joshua said I was a great public speaker, which I will never forget. Those words made me believe I actually was a great speaker. Words are so powerful. We can do a lot for people good and bad with our words. Remember how powerful words (both positive and negative) are when you speak them to others and especially young people. More importantly remember that words only have power over you if you give them power. Before I sat down, Joshua asked me a life-changing question, "What is being in your head costing you?"

I paused to think and became a little sad as I responded, "My Life."

This conversation was a huge wake-up call for me. It was one of the biggest catalysts in beginning the process of figuring out how to get out of my head and into my life.

I encourage you to write (in large print) on a piece of paper and post it on the mirror you look into each morning. "What is living in your head and costing you in your real life?"

The Lifetime channel uses the phrase, "Live Out Loud." I love that! This book will help you bring what's inside of you out to the rest of the world. We all have precious gifts to share with the world but when we are too afraid to share them, no one benefits.

As I began taking action and doing things I never imagined, I decided to reflect upon what got me to this point for two reasons. I finally felt free for the first time in my adult life and I never ever wanted to go back to that place of paralysis—the prison of my own mind. I wanted a blueprint to refer to if I began to backslide or somehow ended up back in that place. Secondly, I hoped that my story might help others find their way out of their head and into action too. Once you have overcome something that is painful to you, you want to help others do the same.

I know how depressing it can feel to be truly paralyzed and the fatigue that results from being stuck in your head without ever taking any action. What helps me now when I catch myself reverting back to my old ways is revisiting all the tips I have written in this book. Hopefully these points will give you the same unstoppable feeling I got then, and continue to get every time I read my own notes. I now know that I can achieve anything I set out to accomplish.

BEGIN READING THE BOOK WITH THIS IN MIND:

Decide in this moment to forgive yourself for all the times you didn't move forward or take action like you wanted.. Most importantly, accept and love yourself right now in this moment for the person you truly are, the person that God has blessed in so many ways. Love yourself for your shortcomings and for your successes because all of it has helped you get to where you are now, but none of it defines you.

Decide in this moment that you are going to take whatever action is needed to become your true and authentic self. Shed the layers that social acceptance has added to your being and slowly begin revealing more of who you really are to the world through your actions.

Taking action need not be scary if you believe your actions are authentic and filled with love. Your actions from this moment forward will not define you but rather you will define your actions. If you take action as an expression of your authentic self, there is no need for fear of failure because the action is not about success or failure, but rather the greatest gift God gave us – self-expression. If you make your actions about expressing your true self entwined with love you can't help but take more and more action.

To get the most out of this book, it should be used as a workbook. Highlight what is important to you, make notes in the margins and/or at the end of each chapter, in the section called KEY POINTS, or on the blank pages (pg. 6, 28, 46, 60). The KEY POINTS section can be used to complete the activities discussed, to document important things you need to work on, things you want to remind yourself to do or to think about etc. Use this section to document whatever is necessary to create action and move yourself forward.

Get Out of Your Head and Into Your Life!

KEY POINTS: (things to do, reminders, thoughts, etc.):

1 Cultivate the Right Attitude

> "Life is 10 percent what happens to me
> and 90 percent how I react to it."
> –Charles Swindoll

Attitude can be defined as the way you think and feel about something or someone. Attitude may be the single biggest factor for your happiness. It's simple really. You can look at your life with disappointment and frustration or hope and gratitude. You can focus on what makes you happy or you can focus on what makes you sad, angry, etc. If you have a challenging situation that can't be changed then you must change how you think about it. If you approach it with a "poor me" attitude, that is how you will continue to feel. In almost every situation you can focus on something good or bad. How you choose to look at things really has a big impact on your health and happiness. So before you read on, do an attitude check for yourself. Is your glass half empty or half full? Are you open to all the good that you can have in your life? Do you look for the good in everything and everyone? Do you focus on something that you're grateful for everyday?

I remember hearing Louise Hay in 101 Power Thoughts for Life say that she looks at paying her bills with gratitude. When I first heard this statement, I thought it sounded a little crazy. As I listened, she started to make sense. She said we have bills because we are able to create them. We have a roof over our head, so we have rent to pay and utility bills. The homeless have no bills and they also do not have shelter. No one likes paying taxes to the government but Louise says to think of them as paying rent to live in the country. America affords us many luxuries that other countries do not. It is the land of opportunity, so thinking of taxes as a way for me to continue to live in my country with all its wonderful benefits makes me feel better about my taxes. Most of us do not think about paying bills with gratitude, but why not? This is just one example of how we can change our attitude.

I became more aware of the power of this attitude shift, when I looked at my own life. I often felt tired and frustrated with my children's poor attention and hyperactivity and I wished that they would be calmer like other children. To this day if I dwell on their negative behavior it frustrates, fatigues, and depresses me. However, I have to remind myself, there are parents of children with mental challenges and disabilities that can't walk, run or even attend school, and here I am not thanking God for the beautiful children I have. When I look at my children for all their wonderful qualities, and accept them just as they are, my happiness increases significantly. My children are the same children, but with a glass-half-full attitude everything is better.

I'm not saying I never have a bad day. I do. But when I do, I reflect on everything I'm grateful for which changes my focus and gives me an attitude adjustment. Attitude can be defined as, "a manner of acting, feeling, or thinking that shows one's disposition, opinion, etc."

We get more of what we focus on. When I focus on the less desirable qualities of my sons, then that's all I see. I feel frustrated and disappointed, even depressed. When I refocus on all the wonderful qualities in my boys, I see more of those qualities. I feel joy, peace, and gratitude.

Your attitude is very powerful. It's your state of mind. You can't control everything that happens in life, but you can certainly control how you react to it. Once you recognize that you are in control of your thoughts and your thoughts create your feelings and your feelings drive your actions, you can see that learning to control your thoughts will greatly impact your level of happiness.

One way you can begin to practice this is to become more aware of your body. Your physical state will help determine if you have strong confident thoughts or weak, doubting thoughts. Think about how you breathe, how you walk, and how you hold your body. If you want to be confident and feel successful, but walk with your head down, shoulders slumped forward with a depressed demeanor, it's hard for your mind to say "success" when your body is saying "failure". Even if you don't feel like smiling or standing straight, begin slowly training yourself. Smiling and proper posture will help create positive feelings. Make a conscious effort to do this for 5 minutes a day then 15 then 30 and so on. If you take up running you will not run 5 miles on your first day. You may run for 15 minutes or a short distance and build up your stamina over weeks and months. This is no different but you have to do the exercises.

In general some form of physical exercise will definitely change your state. Exercise creates energy and momentum. It helps clear our minds. Exercise increases our blood flow and in turn our oxygen levels, which can change the way we are thinking and feeling. Find some form of exercise and make it part of your daily/weekly routine. If you feel the need for an attitude adjustment and you are not able to take a walk or exercise in any way, simply doing some deep breathing can bring more oxygen into the body to help change your state into a more positive one.

Food, appropriate amounts of water, vitamin deficiencies from not eating the right food, sleep and stress also cause chemical reactions in the body that affect our mood and our state of mind. Food can greatly impact our thoughts both positively and negatively. If your diet consists of too much chemically processed junk food and lots of caffeinated sugary beverages, you may feel sluggish, irritable, overwhelmed and/or depressed to varying degrees. When your body feels like this, can you imagine what types of thoughts and attitudes you might produce? They are typically not thoughts of success, happiness and well-being.

Simpler healthier foods lead to simpler healthier thinking. If you drink lots of water, eat a simple diet of whole foods from nature such as fruits and vegetables, bean, legumes, whole grains free from processing and chemicals, you can feel lighter, more energetic, and experience a more peaceful sense of well-being. Try it for a couple months and pay attention to your thoughts during the process. As you simplify and purify your way of eating it may take some time for your body to adjust. As you eat healthier foods, you may experience some detoxifying symptoms, so be patient and know that in time you will feel great.

Exercising, eating healthy food, drinking plenty of water, reducing stress, getting adequate amounts of sleep and positive thoughts are the recipe for a healthy attitude.

■

"Just smiling goes a long way toward making you feel better about life. And when you feel better about life, your life is better."

–Art Linkletter

"What is the difference between an obstacle and an opportunity? Our attitude toward it. Every opportunity has a difficulty, and every difficulty has an opportunity."

–J. Sidlow Baxter

KEY POINTS: (things to do, reminders, thoughts, etc.):

NOTES:

2
Utilize a Good Listener

"An appreciative listener is always stimulating."
—*Agatha Christie*

Listening is a forgotten art. People in today's society ask a question and many times don't even wait for an answer, let alone really listen to what the other person is saying. People are too busy waiting for their turn to talk than listening with any kind of real compassionate presence. Finding someone who can really listen to you is a vital part of taking action in your life. It is through talking and answering questions that we find out the amazing things that lie deep within us.

A great listener is extremely powerful. We are often on automatic pilot and never slow down long enough to recognize our own dysfunction. Many times problems are a manifestation of things deep inside us and figuring out what that issue is can unravel the whole knot. When we deal with issues on the surface and don't address those things deep inside, the real issues, we are functioning somewhat like the current medical system. When someone doesn't feel well, we treat the symptoms with a pill that is supposed to fix the problem. Many times the pill just suppresses the symptoms. The pill works until side effects result from the pill or the underlying problem worsens causing a new set of symptoms and the need for another pill, another Band-Aid. Instead of treating the symptoms, the underlying causes need to be addressed. In many cases, these causes are the way we think, poor diet, lack of exercise, stress, and/or lifestyle.

Overeating, excess weight, alcoholism, time management issues, procrastination, clutter, perfectionism, overachiever, anxious/stressed, workaholic—whatever the issue, they all have lists of how-to's that go along with overcoming them. In some instances, the lists can be thought of as the pills temporarily suppressing the symptoms.

A lot of times you know your own answers deep within but you don't take the time to listen to your inner knowing. Or sometimes you have buried things so deeply that it's difficult to retrieve without help. If you talk to any number of people that want to lose weight they can give you a list of things they need to do. If they did them, they would most likely lose the weight. If you ask a procrastinator, what they should do differently, they can give you a list of the things they should do. If it was that simple, all of us would find the list to fix our problem, follow it and our problems would be gone. But it's not that simple.

How many of you with disorganization or clutter get all fired up to fix the problem? We follow the list to be clutter-free and organized. We clean up everything, buy containers and throw things away just like the list says, only to have the clutter return in a few weeks or even days. How about those of us trying to lose weight? We follow the list of to do's and lose weight only to have the pounds return at some point. Our symptoms are the weight gain, the procrastination, the clutter, the anxiety, the fear and yes, if you follow the list of steps to fix them like taking a pill, the symptoms will go away for a little while. But in time they will resurface or another problem of the same or similar nature shows up. There may be some people who truly don't know how to fix their issues and given a list may be able to follow it and succeed for a lifetime, but the majority of us need to dig deep and figure out the underlying problem.

We need to figure out the experiences that shaped our thoughts and caused us to believe certain ideas about ourselves. We need to figure out the reason why we developed our symptoms (weight, procrastinating, clutter, drinking, time management, anxiety, or you fill in the blank) in the first place. Procrastinating may be a result of growing up wanting everything to be perfect so your parents would love you. Do you work to please everyone because you want to feel loved or are afraid of being abandoned? Do you feel the need to control everything as a result of something that happened in your childhood that you couldn't control? These are just a few thoughts to consider when working on the whole issue of procrastination.

Many of you might have a nagging issue that you can't seem to transcend. There are times when it might be a simple issue that's easy to remedy. Other times, it might be bigger or go deeper. You might need to get clear about why you have developed the issues in the first place. If you can figure out the underlying cause, you can create a lifelong solution to the problem. It may not be a simple fix but once you know the real cause you can begin working with it instead of treating the symptoms. Awareness is the first step to creating change.

I highly recommend a Holistic Health Coach, a life coach, or someone trained in listening and guiding to help you. I am trained as a Holistic Health Coach and have personal experience in using a health coach, so I can tell you it's a guided journey that through listening and asking the right questions can help redirect your thoughts. A coach can help you figure out your formula for a healthy, balanced life and guide you based on your own inner wisdom. Think about it. Who knows yourself better than you do? A coach can step in and based on what you are sharing, help you see what's causing you to be stuck.

If you've seen the movie Star Wars, I relate this kind of coaching to the Jedi's battles and adventures. As they go through their adventures discovering the unknown, they forge on; one discovery at a time making their own decisions and figuring out what they need to do to accomplish their mission. While they seem to be on their own throughout the journey, we know they are guided by the Force. The Force is always with them, challenging them, and helping to unleash their greatest skills and to be the best Jedi they can be. By listening and asking the right questions at appropriate times, Holistic Health Coaches are often able to lead individuals down a path of self-discovery unlike any other.

"Being heard is so close to being loved that for the average person, they are almost indistinguishable."

—David Augsburger

"Inner guidance is heard like soft music in the night by those who have learned to listen."

—Vernon Howard

KEY POINTS: (things to do, reminders, thoughts, etc.):

3 Journal Your New and Good

"Acknowledging the good that you already have in your life is the foundation for all abundance."
—*Eckhart Tolle*

While a student at Integrative Nutrition, I found myself listening to people's success stories and instead of sharing in their happiness or being motivated by their success, I noticed myself feeling sad. I wanted to accomplish the kind of success these people had, but instead my success was still only in one place, my head. I was always busy but didn't have anything great or really big to report like these people or so I thought. I had lots of ideas, but they never turned into anything. The truth is I rarely ever gave any of them a try. Honestly the few ideas I did try never got off the ground because I couldn't get out of my head long enough for them to have a chance.

Isn't this what a lot of us do to ourselves? You look at the difference between where you are in the present moment and where you want to be.

You may even get so excited that you start in the direction of your dream, but before long you feel overwhelmed. You start to think it's too much to accomplish, too far to go or you tell yourself you could never do that. You get sad, discouraged and give up before you even really try.

Well this happened to me a number of times until something changed. I had a lot of motivation from attending Integrative Nutrition where I was learning not just about healthy nutrition but about how to have a healthy, happy life. I was learning a lot, especially about my own issues and I had support from my own health coach and all my fellow students. Instead of reporting only a couple things that I could call to mind when my health coach asked me what was new and good, I decided to begin to journal what was new and good on a regular basis. I included everything I could think of that had improved in my life no matter how small. My first series of new and good was a list that looked like:

1. made dinner with my boys
2. having more positive thoughts
3. exercising more
4. doing better about controlling clutter
5. took a few minutes to meditate

While there was nothing earth shattering in my journal I made sure I listed every little improvement I could think of. Each time I recorded my new and good, I reviewed all of my previous entries. I amazed myself when I realized how many accomplishments I had listed and the progress I'd made.

As I read through the list, I realized many of the improvements were very minor but all were steps forward. As I continued to journal and add to my list, I began to feel a great sense of accomplishment and momentum. I realized that while my new and good didn't include rocking the world, it did include things that were rocking my world and my family's world. I began to feel a huge sense of accomplishment in what I had done to affect change within my own life and my family's life that it gave me confidence and momentum to accomplish more and even begin to take some steps to create some change outside my own little bubble.

I continue to keep lists of what I am achieving and this gives me a sense of accomplishment and gratitude as I reflect and journal each new entry. Journaling is very powerful. It's a way to capture our thoughts, feelings, ideas, and life events. You can get a lot of insight into yourself by reading over past journal entries.

Growth is not always noticed when you are close to it. For instance you may not notice how much your children are changing from year to year, but Aunt Mollie who only visits once a year sees a lot of changes. We live with ourselves every minute of every day and a lot of times hardly notice we've changed. However, when you review your journal entries you will often see tremendous growth and progress that you would not otherwise be able to give yourself credit for.

Writing down what you're thinking is a great first step to getting out of your head. If you don't journal especially your new and good, there is a tendency to focus only on what you have not accomplished yet, what you still want to fix, and where you still want to go. It's fine to look forward, and continuously improve yourself and your world. You must have goals but you also must take time to reflect on your accomplishments, to give yourself a pat on the back, and find gratitude and appreciation for the results you have achieved. If you continuously look to what is still missing, you will probably become discouraged, even sad because there is always improving that can be done. You might even feel like a hamster on a wheel.

Many of us are constantly setting and working to achieve goals. The moment when we actually achieve a goal may be brief while the journey to achieving it may have taken years. With this in mind, it is very important to find a way to enjoy the journey and always celebrate all the goals you do achieve no matter how small. If you don't look at what you've accomplished and reflect on your personal growth, you will never celebrate. It is exactly who you are at any moment in time that helps to shape and bless all those you interact with. Without celebration, you may burn out in the continuous quest to improve and achieve. Celebrate your growth and improvements by journaling your accomplishments often—no matter how big or small. Most importantly don't compare yourself to anyone else. You are unique and no one can compare to you so celebrate who YOU ARE and what YOU have accomplished.

"Always concentrate on how far you've come, rather than how far you have left to go."

—Unknown

"Cultivate the habit of being grateful for every good thing that comes to you, and give thanks continuously. And because all things have contributed to your advancement, you should include all things in your gratitude."

—Ralph Waldo Emerson

KEY POINTS: (things to do, reminders, thoughts, etc.):

_____
_____
_____
_____
_____
_____
_____
_____
_____
_____
_____
_____
_____
_____

4 Shift the Focus of Your Thoughts

"For the things we have to learn before we can do them, we learn by doing them."

—Aristotle

Shifting the focus of my thoughts from Outcome thinking to Action thinking was the most significant key to propel me out of my head and into my life. My first personal test of this method turned out to be my breakthrough action and a major turning point in my life. Up until this point in my life, I was not someone that would speak up about too much. I had a lot of opinions but they stayed in my head. If I had an opinion in a meeting, I would get myself all worked up trying to figure out how to word my comments and when to speak. By the time I "figured it out," it was no longer an appropriate time to speak about it.

So here was my challenge. I wanted to talk to my hospital's CEO about my Holistic Health Coaching practice and ways I could bring my nutrition knowledge to the hospital. When I focused my thoughts on the outcome of asking to meet with my CEO, my thoughts were a stream of questions and doubts that sounded like this:

- How can I meet with the CEO?
- Am I crazy?
- He doesn't know me, so why would he agree to meet with me?
- He is too busy to meet with me.
- What will I say if I do get a meeting?
- He's not going to be interested in Holistic Health.
- I don't know enough to talk to him.
- I haven't prepared enough.
- The thoughts go on and on.

I'm sure you've had similar barrages of negative thoughts about something you've wanted to do that got in the way of your taking action. Instead of these outcome-based thoughts that were coming to mind, I focused only on the action I wanted to take, which was to meet with the CEO. Whenever my thoughts shifted from the action of scheduling and having a meeting with the CEO to the outcome of the meeting: "What if he doesn't want to meet? What if it doesn't go well? What if he's doesn't like what I have to say?" I would dismiss them and not let myself engage in them.

So how did I schedule a meeting with my CEO? I literally did not allow myself to have thoughts about the outcome. If my mind drifted to those thoughts, I immediately redirected them to something else which was usually the actions I needed to take. The actions were simple and something anyone could do. When all else failed, I would focus on my breath, my heartbeat and feel my toes and feet on the ground to stop my thinking.

Thanks to this outcome-focused approach my meeting with the CEO was relaxed and a success in more ways than one. The biggest success was not related to all the details of the meeting but rather in completing the action, having the meeting with the CEO and discussing Holistic Health Coaching. I took the action! The outcome is secondary and much less important. Outcomes will be what outcomes will be, sometimes in spite of our best effort. One thing I have learned related to achieving the outcomes you want is being very clear. The clearer you are about what action steps you want to accomplish, the better your chances of accomplishing them.

I could have planned to talk with him without any real objectives but when I prepared for my meeting I knew there were three points I wanted to discuss and one question I wanted him to answer.

1. Make him aware of Holistic Health
2. Talk about how Holistic Health can impact employee productivity
3. Find out his level of interest for the hospital

The question I asked was, "Could I offer sessions to educate/coach my employees during lunch?" We talked about all these things and even some of his eating habits.

The most important thing to remember is "There can be NO OUTCOME without first taking ACTION."

With this thought in mind, I want to talk about a concept that works for a lot of people. I've been to a number of motivational seminars, read books and heard people say, "Feel the Fear and Do It Anyway." This concept is very successful and has helped many people.

For me this strategy never worked and still doesn't work. It actually produces negative emotions for me because of the bad experiences I had using it. I hope that this new way of thinking unlocks endless possibilities for you because it did for me. I was constantly in my head, playing what I should say or do over and over, like a broken record or a scratched DVD. I would continuously try to come up with the perfect dialogue or the perfect action, so frightened that I might mess things up if I didn't say or do it right. I believed that it was only good if every conversation or action produced the outcome that I wanted. I believed that if I was good enough and did it just right the outcome would be what I wanted and if it wasn't, it was because I wasn't good enough.

I had lots of ideas about what I wanted to happen and when an opportunity presented itself, I would immediately get into my head with those racing thoughts. Those thoughts focused on how to have the perfect outcome. Was the timing right? Was I prepared enough? What if I didn't say the right thing because I hadn't rehearsed? And we can't forget, what will they think of me? All these thoughts led to my heart racing, a lump in my throat and sweaty palms. While all these terrible physical symptoms were manifesting, I was thinking my outcome-based thoughts and mixing in my "feel the fear and do it anyway" thoughts.

In my head it sounded like this: What if the timing is wrong? This is as good of time as any. You really can do it. What if I am not prepared enough? Feel the fear and just do it! The more thoughts I had the more nervous I became. I was definitely feeling the fear as my pulse continued to race, the size of the lump in my throat increased and the clarity of my thinking seemed to almost go numb until my brain literally seized to work. I'd work myself up into a complete panic convincing myself to face my fear and just do it. Often the fear won, and I would convince myself the timing was not right. I'd let myself off the hook and of course lose that opportunity completely because I never opened my mouth.

Other times when I did finally get myself to speak while "feeling the fear," I was usually so worked up and so nervous by the time I opened my mouth what came out was anything but what I wanted to say. It certainly wasn't something confident that could lead me to a successful outcome, which reinforced the fear I had of doing something like this again. Each time I attempted it, I seemed to feel the fear even more intensely as my mind stored more and more of the negative outcomes from the previous attempts to feel the fear and do it anyway. The fear won again and again.

I finally figured out that what I feared was the outcome. So what I did instead of feeling the fear and doing it anyway was stop thinking about the outcome. Would the person be interested in what I had to say? Would they want to buy my services? Would they like me? Am I good enough? Do I know enough? Are they going to think I'm crazy when I share my ideas with them? Blah. Blah. Blah. Forget it. Forget it all. Once I did, the fear faded away. The outcome will be what the outcome will be regardless of your perfect presentation, perfect timing, perfect idea, perfect, perfect, perfect.

When it comes to taking action, perfection is a defense mechanism and a way of procrastinating. Why do we procrastinate? We fear the outcome. Why do we think it has to be just right? We fear the outcome. I am not saying to forget about preparation, practice or to not do your homework. What I am saying is, complete and absolute knowledge, perfect preparation, perfect delivery are not the answers. Perfection in many situations is an impossible concept because perfection is subjective and in the eyes of the beholder. You can throw a perfect party and most people will rave about the experience but inevitably there will be someone that has negative things to say or not like the experience. Their negative experience in reality may have little to do with your party. It may be more about something they are dealing with or insecurities they have acquired over the years or maybe they didn't like it. We are all different and that's OK.

We are all unique. However, if you remain true to who you are inside and speak and do things from your heart, you will feel much better about your outcomes. If it was meant to be, it will be.

I used to strive for my delivery of ideas and information to be perfect. When things didn't work out I used to think it was because I must have done something wrong. I didn't say it the right way or I didn't do it right. I completely overlooked the possibility that there might not have been anything I could have done that would have made the person interested in what I had to say. We all have our own agenda and interests and it often differs from others. It's like trying to sell a lifelong vegetarian some of the best meat ever. It doesn't matter what you say, how you say it or what you tell them about the meat, they won't be interested. This is not to say that people never change their mind about things but I think awareness and synchronicity play a bigger role. Favorable outcomes are more likely to occur when you're taking actions at synchronistic times. I will talk more about that later.

So what I began doing was detaching myself completely from the outcome and focusing my thoughts only on the action I wanted to take. When I scheduled the meeting with my CEO, I had no idea if he was going to like anything I had to say but my victory was in the accomplishment of having the meeting, in taking the action, not in the outcome of the action. I celebrated taking the action and that is what you must celebrate. Find joy and reward yourself for taking action! Without action you have no chance at all to have any result let alone the results you desire.

When the outcome is good you get a bonus. When you eliminate the pressure of wanting or expecting a specific outcome from the action you're taking, you are free to act and be yourself leaving the outcome up to God (the synchronicity of the Universe). So I will say it again, do not think about the outcome. Outcome thinking has a place and I will discuss it more during your goal setting and visualization section.

When you are taking action, if you don't think about the outcome you will not generate the same sense of fear. Imagine you have decided to bungee jump from an extremely high tower. You will likely get a feeling of fear or at least some butterflies, and if you don't get the feeling right away you will surely get it once you reach the top of the tower. Now look at where is the fear coming from. It's probably the outcome of the jump, right? I'm up so high. What if I fall? What if the cord breaks? Could I die? What if it hurts my back? Will I bang into those nearby buildings?

If you don't allow yourself to think at all about the outcomes, you will most likely not feel fear in the same way. People who have a fear of flying don't fear flying itself. They fear the outcomes. They imagine the plane crashing, never seeing their family again, or not having enough oxygen to breathe. If they truly did not engage in thinking about the what ifs related to the outcome of their plane ride, they would not experience the fear and anxiety that their thoughts produce.

Focus your thoughts only on the action you want to take and the steps or process you must follow to accomplish those actions. When I focused on outcome thinking, it was easy for me to think I might not be capable of meeting with my CEO and begin to feel a lot of anxiety and fear. If I had let that thinking take over, I probably would never have scheduled the meeting or I might have tried to cancel it.

Shifting to my Action or Process thinking looked like this:

Goal: Meet with CEO to discuss Holistic Health and coaching my employees

The Process or Action Steps needed to accomplish this:

1. Look up the CEO secretary's phone number.
2. Dial the number.

3. Ask his secretary for a meeting date.
4. Mark my calendar.
5. Review what I want to talk about.
6. On the meeting day, walk to his office.
7. Talk with CEO.

Reviewing each step by itself, easily demonstrates that I, like most of the population, was very capable of completing the steps. Breaking the goal down into individual action steps and looking at each step without any thought except that which was needed to take the action, made accomplishing it quite simple instead of a huge stress-producing ordeal. TAKE ACTION! One action step builds confidence and momentum to taking more and more action. It really feels good, and it was a lot less tiring to just take action than to keep thinking about it and thinking about it.

So what actions do you want to take?

What is your life's purpose?

What are you all about?

■

"Nothing is so fatiguing as the eternal hanging on of an uncompleted task."

–William James

"Inaction breeds doubt and fear. Action breeds confidence and courage. If you want to conquer fear, do not sit around and think about it. Go out and get busy."

–Dale Carnegie

KEY POINTS: (things to do, reminders, thoughts, etc.):

5

Find Your Passion

"We have all been placed on this earth to discover our own path, and we will never be happy if we live someone else's idea of life."

–*James Van Praagh*

Once I realized that I could take any action I wanted, it became clear that I needed to figure out what I really wanted to do with my life. I have always been a dreamer, so ideas came easily to me. If you have never allowed yourself to dream this needs to be your first step. Let your mind go wherever it wants. Don't censor yourself.

Dream as if you were a child again. If you ask a small child what they want to be when they grow up, they might say something like, I want to be a doctor or a pro basketball player. If a child is young enough, they don't say I want to be a doctor but I'm not smart enough, or I want to be a pro basketball player but I might not be tall enough.

Our society tends to shoot down dreams. We tell others, including our children, that they're not good enough. You might not say those exact words but that's the message you send. You help them find all the reasons why it can't be done. We all have a tendency to gravitate toward the negative. Why do we do that? Most of us need continuous feedback and reinforcement to believe we are good at something, to believe we can achieve something or to believe the good things about ourselves. Once you get to the point where you have a good idea or think you can be good at something, you often move forward. Then one person might say something negative or something contrary to what you thought, and you believe it as simple as that. Sometimes you are the person saying the negative things. Many of us are harder on ourselves than anyone else.

This negative thinking does not have to be your reality. You and only you can decide what words and what experiences you internalize. You are the one who chooses to give thoughts meaning or to dismiss them. Dismissing comments, opinions and attitudes that do not serve you, even if they are your own, is as easy as you choose to make it.

If you had a business idea and a four- year-old told you it wouldn't work, you'd laugh and most likely go about your plans as usual not giving much thought to their comment. You can do this in any situation with anyone's comments but you have to be aware and realize its happening. Often our first instinct is to believe the negative, especially if it's pointing to one of our insecurities. Remember, if something was true at one point, it doesn't have to be true now. If you were not a good public speaker in high school, it doesn't mean you can't be a good one now or in the future. Look out for those self-defeating, negative thoughts and dismiss them. In order to do that, stay clear about why you want to do something. Your "why" will serve as your unwavering, unfaltering determination. The best thing you can do is figure out what you want out of life, and most importantly what you want to contribute to the world.

Before we create goals for our lives we need to ask a few questions.

- Does what I am doing each day bring me passion and excitement?
- Does it light my fire?
- Does it excite me to talk about it?
- Is it something that keeps me up at night or makes me jump out of bed in the morning?

Find Your Passion

Think about who you are deep down inside. Who is that person you really want to be? If you could wave a magic wand and be your ideal self at this moment in time, what would you stand for? What type of character do you have? What personal gifts and talents do you want to share with the world?

Define who you are or who you want to be on paper. Think about your passions and develop your mission statement or your life's purpose and put it in writing. Your mission statement should be a clear representation of your purpose for existence. The Institute for Integrative Nutrition's mission is, "to play a crucial role in improving health and happiness in America and through that process, create a ripple effect that transforms the world." The mission of Google is, "to organize the world's information and make it universally accessible and useful." The Lance Armstrong Foundation has a mission, "to inspire and empower people with cancer to live strong."

As you create your mission statement and begin developing your goals, take time to reflect on what you really need for happiness. By this I don't mean for anyone to think that a goal must be achieved in order to be happy. Happiness comes from within and is a choice, more like a state of being. What I mean is what things feed your soul? What things can you do that help you express who you are and what are those things that excite you? If you can't follow your passions in your career choice, can you add it into your life in other ways? Find something in your current job that you are passionate about to focus on. If you are having trouble figuring out what you are passionate about, don't feel bad. Many of us have been caught up in the day to day and have not thought about it for years. For me I have become very passionate about the things I've overcome. A Chinese Proverb says, "the obstacle is the way." Now, whenever I am struggling, I try to understand it and figure out what good is supposed to come of it. What lessons can I to learn from my struggles and how can I use what I've learned to help others?

Years ago, during what felt like the darkest time in my life, I experienced a life-changing lesson. I was dealing with my son's chronic sickness for his first four years of life. He was diagnosed constantly with ear, sinus and respiratory infections, allergies, reflux, hyperactivity, night terrors and was on medicine for breathing. I felt very sad, anxious and even depressed. I remember praying all the time. I tried not to ask why but couldn't help but think it sometimes. I continued to pray not only for my son's return to health, but for my deeper understanding of the situation, so I could help.

As it turned out, his sickness led me to research nutrition and its effects on illness. I began changing my son's diet. To make a long story short, he is no longer on any medication. He's only been to see his pediatrician a handful of times and most of those visits were for regular school check-ups. In the process of researching nutrition for my son's health, I found and attended Integrative Nutrition. I developed a very deep passion for educating others and have been developing a different career path related to this ever since. This career is much different than my management job which I like in some ways, but am not as passionate about.

My new passions fill me with excitement. I have found ways to incorporate some of the things I am passionate about in my management job. It's ironic that the darkest time in my life has completely transformed my life. I am so grateful for that time now. I didn't understand when I was going through it but it deepened my spiritual life and led me to one of my passions in life. I would never guess that something so good could come out of something that felt so bad. Keep this in mind as you go through your struggles in life. Try to look at how your situation is making you a stronger, better person.

If you are not sure what you are passionate about, think of the obstacles you have overcome in your life or pay attention to what you love to do. Once you bring your passions into focus use them to help you construct your mission statement and corresponding goals. Most importantly, do not dismiss any goals because they don't seem possible. A lot of things are possible, if you make them happen one action step at a time and believe.

■

"Find out who you are and do it on purpose."

—Dolly Parton

KEY POINTS: (things to do, reminders, thoughts, etc.):

NOTES:

6 Pursue Your Goals with Child-Like Persistence

"Our goals can only be reached through a vehicle of a plan, in which we must fervently believe, and upon which we must vigorously act. There is no other rout to success."

–*Pablo Picasso*

Have you ever observed a child who wants something? Maybe it's a toy, or to visit a friend, or go out in the snow. Whatever it may be, when they want something they will not stop asking you for it. You wonder where they get the energy or how they could possibly ask the same question so many times without accepting the answer no. They keep at you. As parents, we teach our children over time that when they ask and we say no that's enough. Don't ask again, once asked is enough right? We said no. No means no, so stop asking.

As children, we start out with a strong pursuit of the things we want in life and are relentless in obtaining them. Our parents, teachers, aunts and uncles teach us that no is no and to quit asking. We take this thinking into our adult lives. It's why so many of us don't succeed at the levels we desire. We need to get back into our childlike mode of endless persistence. If you have a good understanding of why you want to achieve a goal, you can create a clear picture of the goal and develop a strong commitment to it.

When you read the biographies of great historical figures who have achieved amazing success and accomplished great things, you will discover that they started out with an idea that no one listened to, people didn't like or even thought was crazy. Keep this in mind as you dream and map out your goals.

When I decided to map out my goals, I used a system created by Frank Gasiorowski, at the time. It used a series of emails to walk me through a process for setting and achieving goals in 90 days. It was very helpful because it gave me a lot of things to think about as I was doing this exercise for the first time. The step-by-step system moved me through the process and helped me start writing things down. If you are not familiar with setting goals there are a lot of good resources that can walk you through the process in more detail.

You may think you know what you want to accomplish but have never thought about in terms of what you really enjoy. So many of us get caught up in the daily to do's that we have no idea what really gets us excited or how to make our passions an integral part of our life. If circumstances prevent you from taking steps now to move toward your future dream goals, it is very important to find joy and passion in your current life.

Here's how to start: Begin by describing your goals on paper in as specific terms as you can. Putting your goals in writing helps clarify them, bring them into focus, and make them real. Record action steps and deadlines with each goal.

Now is the time to think about the outcomes. Think about what you want to accomplish—your outcomes. Work backward to figure out the steps you must take to get there. Another way to say this is start with the end in mind. Work backward by year, by month, by week, by day and by hour of the day so that you have detailed action steps with deadlines to accomplish your dreams. I cannot stress deadlines enough. While we might miss a deadline here or there, we need them to keep us moving along.

Goals without time-lines have a tendency to get stuck. This point is especially important for the procrastinators. If you do not set deadlines, nothing will happen because you will just keep procrastinating. Sit down with a planner and make schedules, set deadlines and try to be very diligent about keeping them but make sure they are realistic.

Also be mindful that we often have to grow personally and in our professional skills before we can achieve our final goals. As you plan your action steps, if growth, training and/or learning needs to take place along the way make sure you specifically put that into your action steps with deadlines.

I can't stress enough the importance of taking action. You can study all the techniques, learning videos and strategies on how to hit a baseball but until you get out there and start swinging at live pitches you'll never know if you can hit a ball let alone get really good at hitting one. You can read cookbook after cookbook but until you get into the kitchen and start making the recipes you will never become a good cook. You don't need to know how to do everything or even have any experience to get started. The majority of people who are great at something had a time when they first began. They were not great the first time they did it and many weren't even good, but through consistent action (practice) they evolved into greatness.

Don't hold yourself back from moving forward because you think you don't have enough experience, enough training, or enough knowledge. Sometimes you just need to get started and then more importantly keep moving forward. Don't stop when you hit those initial bumps in the road and you can anticipate some bumps. It's only natural to make some adjustments. Make them and keep right on going.

Someone else I found incredibly helpful was motivational speaker, Mike Litman (www.MikeLitman.com). He talked about finding your passion and sharing your talents and he really got me thinking about my life differently. He helped me realize I was just going through the motions of life and not really living passionately. He says, "You don't have to get it right you just have to get it going."

It's been a challenge for me, but each day I get a little better at just getting things going and not worrying about if I know enough or am good enough. His philosophy is right on. Successful people take action.

I'm not saying they don't have fears but they still put things into action, fix, improve, and learn from their mistakes as they go.

Successful people understand that being told no is a necessary part of being successful. You can't truly fail unless you quit or worse yet if you never try. I think somehow I had convinced myself that if I didn't try at all, it somehow didn't count as failure or rejection. What nonsense! I believe the far greater failure is not for those who have tried and failed, but for those who live safe in our own minds. People who live their lives in their heads never get to experience failure, alternative opportunities, or synchronicity. They don't get to experience much at all because they are too afraid that things might not work out the way they want. The problem with being stuck in your head is it's really hard to fix, improve upon or lead to something better when no one other than you knows what you are thinking. We all have great gifts to share with the world, but we can't share them by living in our heads.

When you are determining your goals and what you want out of life, develop them with an attitude of service towards others. How can your passion serve others, solve their problems, and make their life better? Once I started paying attention to service, I noticed that more breakthroughs came out of helping someone else. I noticed that when my focus was solely on me getting everything I wanted, things just didn't seem to move along the same way. When my focus was on helping others, making a difference, sharing my gifts and expressing myself, I was able to make the most progress toward my goals. So get clear on what you are passionate about and figure out how you can use your passion to fill a need and to help others as you develop your goals.

In Summary, here is a breakdown of how to pursue your goals:
- Create your vision.
- Make a master list of what you want to accomplish.
- Prioritize your list into a small more focused list
- Take your focused list and map out action steps.
- If something is difficult, break it down into the smallest steps that you can do. (This may mean you have action steps that involve learning how to do something or hiring someone to do it)

- Be very specific about each action step.
- Add deadlines to each step.
- Designate days and times to work on your action steps/goals/planning.
- Schedule time to work on the action steps you have mapped out.
- Focus on one step at a time. Looking too far ahead can be overwhelming.
- Don't wait until you feel like it.
- Watch out for excuses and make sure you build milestones into your goals so that you reward yourself for your achievements.
- Do it. Take action.
- Follow through on what you have written.
- Celebrate your accomplishments along the way
- Take consistent action.
- Create a consistent routine of planning, scheduling, goal setting, and reviewing and updating it all.

Don't forget! Set aside time to work on your steps and the things that are most important to you, or you will inevitably spend your entire life doing things that need to be done, laundry, dishes, mowing the grass, cleaning, grocery shopping and never working on those things that are really important to you.

■

"It's not who you are that holds you back, it's who you think you're not."

—Author Unknown

"The greater danger for most of us lies not in setting our aim too high and falling short; but in setting our aim too low, and achieving our mark."

—Michelangelo

KEY POINTS: (things to do, reminders, thoughts, etc.):

_____
_____
_____
_____
_____
_____
_____
_____
_____
_____
_____
_____
_____
_____
_____
_____
_____

Goal Blockers

After you have your goals detailed down to the day, you should be well on your way to accomplishing them. Writing them out in great detail will give you amazing focus. Watch out for things that can distract you from accomplishing your goals. Don't allow those negative thoughts to creep in and tell you can't do something. If you don't think you have enough confidence, remember you gain confidence by doing, not by thinking about doing. Don't let fear stop you.

Fear can definitely be a goal blocker if you let it. One of my favorite pieces of writing is by Marianne Williamson. I first heard it in the movie Coach Carter. I loved it when I heard it and was reminded of it in some of the materials I received at Integrative Nutrition. I think of it when I am not using my talents.

Our Deepest Fear

"Our deepest fear is not that we are inadequate. Our deepest fear is that we are powerful beyond measure. It is our light, not our darkness that most frightens us. We ask ourselves, who am I to be brilliant, gorgeous, talented, fabulous?

Actually, who are you not to be?

You are a child of God. Your playing small does not serve the world. There is nothing enlightened about shrinking so that other people won't feel insecure around you. We are all meant to shine, as children do. We were born to make manifest the glory of God that is within us. It is not just in some of us; it is everyone. And as we let our own light shine, we unconsciously give other people permission to do the same. As we are liberated from our own fear, our presence automatically liberates others."

(Excerpted from A Return to Love: Reflections on the Principles of a Course in Miracles, by Marianne Williamson, HarperCollins Publishers)

Disorganization and clutter are specific blocks. If things are not progressing the way you would like, reflect on your surroundings. Are they full of clutter, piles, and disorganization or do things seem neat, orderly and flow freely? Consider doing some de-cluttering and organizing of your physical space whenever you get stuck. Cleaning out closets is a good place to start. By letting go of the old stuff, you release old stuck energy and make room for new things in your life. At the very least you'll have more room in your closet and feel good about accomplishing something.

Our physical surrounding is often reflective of what is going on internally. Do you keep a lot of things you don't need? Do you collect information and never do anything with it? Remember you will always be able to find what you need when you need it. When you read and collect information for everything, you are wasting precious time. It's a distraction and a form of procrastination. If you like to collect information and just can't do without general information surfing, have a designated place to store it. Schedule and limit your time for it, but don't allow yourself to go beyond the boundaries you've set including the amount of physical space you are using to store it.

Time management can be another block to achieving our goals. Most of us want to achieve our goals but can't understand why we never have time. It's often not that we don't have time it's that we are not using our time for the right tasks. If you find you do not have time to work on your goals, then you are not managing your time appropriately. We all have the same amount of time each day. If you reflect on your days, I'm sure you're doing something that can wait. Become a planner and find a good time management system and schedule all of your time. If you don't plan, you will constantly be trying to figure out what needs to done next. You will also end up doing things that take up your time but are not what's most important. This is very draining and keeps you from enjoying life and being open to all opportunities.

Scheduling your most important to do's helps you to say no to those things that are not aligned with your goals. If you schedule the most important things at the beginning of the week, they will get done and some of the not so important things may have to wait. At the very least scheduling allows you to make a conscious choice to say yes or no to your goals at any moment. Studies show that most of our results come from 20% of our efforts. If you are constantly busy but never accomplishing anything, you need to start planning or reevaluate your current method of planning. Instead of trying to do everything, do only the things that will yield the biggest results.

When planning activities related to your goals you want to look at several things. Schedule what is most important to you first! Then look at your other to dos. How much of your time is something going to take and what kind of results do you expect to obtain? This kind of questioning will help you decide which activities will be the most productive for you.

You've probably heard about the experiment with the rocks and sand. Well, I'm going to remind you again. In this experiment, you take a bowl, add water then sand, then small rocks. When you get to the big rocks, which represent the things that are most important, they don't fit in the bowl. If you repeat the experiment and begin with the large rocks, then the small rocks, then the sand and finally the water it all fits. Such is life. If you do not schedule the most important things, they will never get done. When you schedule those most important things, the other have to's still get done.

Let's talk a little more about scheduling. Have you ever noticed how every time you leave early for an appointment everything runs smoothly but when you leave even a little bit late you get behind the slowest driver on the planet, a detour, a train, you name it, but it all goes wrong? If you plan and organize your time, you will begin to see that you have more of it. When you have little windows of free time and are clear about what needs to be done, you will more often choose to knock those items off your to-do list instead of waiting until the last minute. Instead of driving 20 minutes to make a special trip to the store for that present or for the eggs that you need for tonight's dinner, you will have picked up the present when you are out and passing the store or the eggs when you made your scheduled trip to the grocery store for all the ingredients you need to make this week's meals that you planned.

Initially I resisted this kind of planning in my life. I was a free spirit. I didn't want to live by some rigid plan and I didn't. The problem was I never had a plan so I always felt behind and life seemed to be leading me. When I did try and relax, I always felt like I should be doing something else.

I have not mastered planning and scheduling yet but I will. I have already seen huge improvements in my stress levels, the amount I am able to accomplish, and the control I feel I have over my time. In the past, I never had time to do anything related to my goals. Now I accomplish more than I have in my life and I attribute much of that to planning, organization, and scheduling/time management. I will continue to work on mastering these skills because I know they will help me make the best use of my day. We only have 24 hours in a day—even the president of the United States. How efficiently are you using them?

Complexity is another block. In today's world, nothing is simple. We have 25 brands for every product. We can even make getting dressed a project if we want. We participate in so many activities and so do our children. It's the way of the world now; more is better. We have to be it all, do it all and have it all. Don't get caught up in all this hype and consumerism. Keep things simple. Less is better. Keep that thought in mind when you are reflecting on your life. Is there anything you are spending lots of time on that doesn't align with your goals? What areas of your life can simplify?

A less obvious way of being distracted from our goals is watching TV or using the internet (surfing, Facebook). Everyone watches TV, so it's OK. It's a normal part of life. Right? TV can be an escape from doing or dealing with the things in your life that you don't look forward to or enjoy. It lets you escape into a fantasyland. It's another way of living in your head. You have to recognize it and realize that you can watch life on TV or you can live it. If you are not willing to completely give up your TV, I would set strict limits on how many hours of TV you allow yourself to watch in a day or week and what you watch. Pick a favorite show or two and turn it off otherwise. If you are not diligent, it will steal your time without you realizing it and take you away from moving forward in achieving your goals. The internet can be a powerful tool with a lot of good but like the TV, you must be conscious of how you use it and how much time you spend on non-productive activities. Most importantly, if you are going to watch TV, surf the internet, use Facebook, schedule the time you will spend on these activities and stick to your schedule.

Another block to accomplishing our goals is waiting until we feel motivated. If we wait for the right feeling we may never get anything done. We all have ups and down and good and bad days. It can be challenging to make changes so you might not feel that motivated to stretch your comfort zone. Be careful not to mistake talking about what you are going to do with actually doing it. When we talk about doing things we can feel a false sense of accomplishment. Be aware of this and try to do something each day to move forward whether you feel like it or not. Hold yourself accountable. Reference your goal planning action steps often and your vision and dreams even more often. Look at what must be done for the day. At the end of each day, take a few minutes to review what you have accomplished and what you need to accomplish tomorrow. Set your intentions for tomorrow and plan your action steps. Write them down. Don't let yourself do a lot of thinking around the actions you need to take. Don't attach emotions to accomplishing them just record them as a "to do" and complete them. Hold yourself accountable for completing the designated action steps each day. Celebrate as you place a done check mark next to each item you've completed on your list. As you accomplish even small tasks, you will begin to feel more and more motivated.

Guilt is an emotion that can eat away at our energy and well-being. It can be very counterproductive so be careful not to allow thoughts that create that emotion. Regardless if you've done something you shouldn't or haven't done something you should, feeling guilty will not help the situation. Instead of dwelling on those negative thoughts and letting them paralyze you, figure out the action steps needed to move you in a positive direction and take them.

Don't let other people stand in the way of your progress. You may have many people in your life who challenge you or make it difficult to achieve your goals—but only if you let them. You have the power to decide how you will react to what they are saying and doing and what you think about it. Stay focused on what you want to achieve and keep your thoughts in check. Do not allow your thoughts to be negative. You can achieve anything you set your mind to achieve. The key is setting your mind to it and don't let anyone or anything get in your way.

I remember Mike Litman talking about Arnold Schwarzenegger's book, "The Education of a Body Builder." He had his sights fixed on winning it all and being Mr. Olympia. His father passed away and he did not leave the country or break his training to attend his funeral because he felt that it would be a setback and he did not want to risk it. As cold as it seemed, it shed a great deal of light on his unwavering focus on his goal and his determination to achieve it. While I'm sure his father's death touched his heart, he did not allow it to affect his action steps for accomplishing his dream. He was very, very clear on what those action steps were and what he needed to do to accomplish his goal.

The clearer you are and the more defined you make your action steps, the easier it is to not waiver. When goals are abstract, it's easier to let others take up your time, invade space in your mind, allow negative thoughts to affect you etc. Stay focused. Surround yourself with positive supportive people. Limit your contact when possible with those individuals that drain you of your energy and vision. If you live with them, the best thing you can do is stay determined, focused, and clear about your actions steps and when you will complete them. Give no value to negative comments. Take time to meditate and pray and remain true to who you are.

By achieving your goals you are becoming more of the person you want to be—the person you were meant to be. As you become this new person, you might notice some people around you may not want to see you change. They may not be ready for change in their own life and your change may affect their world especially if you spend a good deal of time with them. They may say and do things that sabotage your progress and dissuade you from pursuing your goals. People often make comments and give advice based on their own fears and insecurities. Be mindful of this habit. When you are faced with obstacles, look for the purpose and lesson they are trying to teach you. Most importantly don't allow others to stop you from being a better person and achieving your dreams.

■

"Try this bracelet. If it fits you, wear it. But if it hurts you, throw it away no matter how shiny."

—Kenyan proverb

"It's not enough to be busy; so are ants. The question is: what are we busy about?"

—Henry David Thoreau

KEY POINTS: (things to do, reminders, thoughts, etc.):

_____
_____
_____
_____
_____
_____
_____
_____
_____
_____
_____
_____
_____

7 Use Your Talents to Help Others

"When we give cheerfully and accept gratefully,
we are all blessed."

–Maya Angelou

I have heard that you get what you put out. Some call it Karma, the Buddhist belief that whatever you do comes back to you. I don't know if I really believed it until I saw it happening to me. As a holistic health coach and educator, there have been numerous occasions where I have told someone I would research healing foods for a medical condition and in the process have discovered some very valuable information for myself or for my own family. I went to a breast cancer fundraiser and met someone that enhanced my business through our relationship. I would have never known this person had I not attended the fundraiser. Once I began paying attention to this phenomenon, it was amazing how many times I received just as much in return from my giving.

When you are in a rut, one of the hardest things to do is help others but it's the best time to do it. It will not only help you to feel good by helping someone but more than likely good things will follow. What's more challenging is to recognize and accept that if we are in a rut, we have most likely put ourselves there with our thoughts and actions. Did you ever wake up late and put yourself in a bad mood because you're starting the day behind schedule? You say to yourself, "This is going to be a bad day." One thing after the next happens and of course you say, "I knew this was going to be a bad day!" It's probably not all coincidence. The next time this happens try taking a minute to just stop and think of all the wonderful things you have in your life and try and put it all in perspective and see if your day doesn't turn out different.

I had a rough period in my marriage and honestly didn't think it would last. The funny thing was I think a lot of it was my fault. Of course, I didn't feel like that then. Every day I expected my husband to speak poorly to me, to get angry at something, to make me feel bad and to just pretty much be a bad husband. Then on top of this I would complain about him and what he did every day to a good friend. So I ask you where were my thoughts about my husband? All negative thoughts and that's exactly what I got. At one point, I really considered leaving but I hated for my two boys who were 5 and 3 at the time to not be able to see their father regularly. But I didn't know if I could continue to live that way.

The definition of insanity is doing the same thing over and over expecting different results. One day I was reflecting on this and realized I was insane when it came to my relationship. I decided that if I was not going to do anything about what I didn't like then I needed to stop looking at all the negative and find something good about my husband and my marriage. So I stopped talking to my friend about everything he said and did that I didn't like. I started thinking about all the things I loved about him and the reasons I married him. I began looking at him with compassion and how could I help him during the times when he was upset. I thought about what I could do to make life better for him. As a very small start, I began thanking him for the things he did that I appreciated no matter how small they may have seemed. I also would thank him for being considerate and helpful for even the smallest thing and tried to accept and appreciate him for who he was and not who I wanted him to be. I would ask him what I could do for him especially after he would get upset. Instead of fighting with him as I previously would have done, I would ask if there was anything that was bothering him and what I could do to help. I remember author Louise Hay saying something about relationships and the part we ourselves play. She said if you are not getting what you want out of your relationship look at yourself and what you're doing. Are you doing and saying all the things that you would want from your mate and if not this is where you need to start.

When I began doing this more, something way beyond my imagination happened: he slowly started becoming more the person I had always hoped he would be. It was almost like when I stopped thinking about and dwelling on all his mistakes and negative qualities, they started to disappear and more of the good qualities that I had been thinking about appeared. The more I tried to help him and be thoughtful and considerate of his feelings; the more he mirrored back to me the same loving consideration.

Now the question I ask you is, where did all these bad things that my husband did go? Did they disappear or was I just focused on something else like his good qualities and so I didn't notice them as much anymore?

What I suspect happens often in some marriages with problems is a shift in focus. During the dating period much focus is on physical attraction, and what has drawn you together, and not as much focus on each other's negative aspects. After we marry or are in a relationship for some time we slowly begin to change our focus to the things we dislike or want changed. Our focus shifts from how wonderful our partner is and how we can make them happy to what have you done for me lately? It becomes all about us. If all of the focus is on ourselves, who are we helping? At first, it's just a little and then it becomes more focused on the things we dislike as if all the attention will make it change or go away.

You do this same thing with problems in your life too. You focus and dwell on what's not going right and what you want to change, when you could be focusing on what is going well, your strengths, and your new future. Have you noticed when you feel good and everything is going well, good things just keep happening? Then something negative or bad throws you off track and things go in the other direction and one bad thing after another keeps happening in your life. If you examine your thoughts during those times, you would find they correspond with what's happening in your life. Your thoughts are helping the situation along good or bad. So find a way to help others and keep your thoughts positive and good.

Opportunities to help others are all around us. How we can help will become clear as soon as we take a break from focusing on our own issues and start listening to others. On the other hand keeping your thoughts positive and good can be a challenge because you have years of bad thinking habits to break. Until you train your mind to think more positively the best thing you can do is stay alert. When you catch yourself thinking a negative thought replace it with a positive one. For example while I'm writing this book, I have thoughts like "hundreds of thousands of books are already out there, why would people want to read mine?" When I recognize this record playing in my head, I start thinking about the positives. I am a unique person and have my own way of delivering great information. I love writing so regardless if anyone likes it, it's a great way to express my thoughts. The information in my book is valuable and should be shared with the world. When you find that things are not going the way you'd like, reexamine your service to others and your thoughts.

■

"The best way to find yourself is to lose yourself in the service of others."

–Mahatma Gandhi

"If you light a lamp for somebody, it will also brighten your path."

–Buddha

"I've learned that people will forget what you said, people will forget what you did, but people will never forget how you made them feel."

–Maya Angelou

Use Your Talents to Help Others

KEY POINTS: (things to do, reminders, thoughts, etc.):

NOTES:

8 Create Affirmations

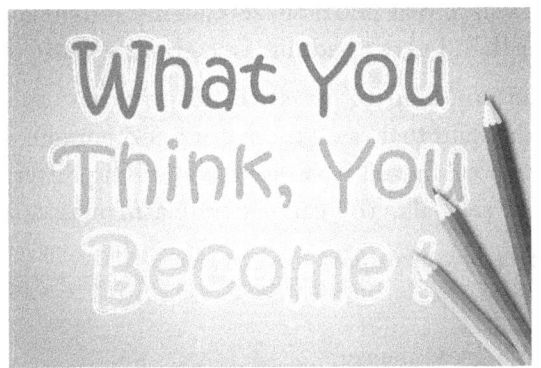

"Dwelling on the negative simply contributes to its power."
—*Shirley Maclaine*

"Affirmations are statements going beyond the reality of the present into the creation of the future through the words you use in the now."
—*Louise L. Hay*

You can set all the goals you want, but if you don't believe in yourself or that you can achieve them, you won't. Affirmations are a way to train your mind to believe you already are what you aspire to be. Think of it as a way to have your mind, fake it until you make it. Affirmations help you put your mind into a state of being instead of a state of wanting and feeling like you'll never have it. Like your goals, there is magic in writing down and reciting your affirmations. Affirmations change your thoughts and your thoughts drive your feelings and create much of your life experience.

You can start with what you say to yourself. Stop talking yourself out of doing things you want with negative self-talk. Have you ever had a really bad experience with a rude person and continued to have conversations in your head about the whole thing for some time after the incident? Or maybe you will re-play and analyze a situation over and over. I did this for a lot longer than I care to admit. Talk about a waste of time.

Don't let any kind of negative self-talk take up space in your brain especially the kind that says you're not good enough, smart enough, don't know enough or should have done something differently. Build yourself up with your self-talk. You can generate affirmations easily.

Here are a few examples:

- I am a great speaker.
- I am healthy and happy.
- I am organized.
- I'm so smart.
- I have an abundance of physical and mental energy.
- I look and feel great.

When a negative thought creeps in (and it will), catch it and create a positive one to say instead.

Becoming aware of your negative self-talk is the first step to changing it.

I'm so tired…I'm vibrant and full of energy.

I'm so fat…I'm beautiful/handsome and eating healthier every day.

There is not enough time in a day…I have all the time I need to accomplish what is important.

Create Affirmations

You don't have to believe what you are saying when you first start but you should choose positive statements that you want to be true. You want to have something positive to say to distract you mind from the negative thoughts. Say your affirmations in the present and keep saying them until they become true.

I found a lot of help from the website: *bestaffirmations.com* with Dr. Patricia Ross. I heard her do a radio interview some time ago and my interpretation of what she said in her talk was this:

A goal is a decision to do something…but then we have all this negative stuff, so you have to keep doing the affirmations. Visualizations are the pictures that go with the affirmations. Visualization continually puts the picture of the ideal thing that you want to happen in front of you. It's like the affirmation but instead of hearing and thinking what you want, you're seeing and thinking it. You have to have goals. Writing your goals down makes them real. We think in mental images. We attract what we think about. Use your senses to make dreams come true.

Dr. Ross uses self-talk in a positive way. She asks, "What comes first, the goal or the affirmation?" She believes the goal comes first and you may not be able to achieve it if you have the wrong mindset. Negative self-talk often causes the wrong mindset. Your thoughts create your reality! Self-talk is quite powerful, and the power is negative or positive depending on the self-talk that you use.

> Definition of affirmation: to affirm means to assert that something is true.

You create your future now. Affirmations help you believe. They help you stay in the right frame of mind. So to move in the direction of your goals, you need to focus on doing positive affirmations. This action changes your thinking so you are only concentrating on the good stuff and not the bad stuff. When you speak affirmations, they can change your thought patterns. You always want to say them in the present tense. Make your affirmation as if it's happening now. "I make a million dollars." This statement might not be true today, but you are creating that mindset. The intention is that it's happening and then one day you will find that it is happening.

Louise Hay has wonderful affirmations too and she is a great resource for learning more about how to create them. I have one of her books and one of her CD's and they have helped me a lot with my thinking.

My formula for "FAKE IT UNTIL YOU MAKE IT" is:

Write it, Say it, Think it until you Believe it and you will Achieve it.

■

"Whether you think that you can or that you can't, you are usually right."

—Henry Ford

"Any thought that is passed on to the subconscious often enough and convincingly enough is finally accepted."

—Robert Collier

"I can do everything through him who gives me strength."

—Philippians 4:13

KEY POINTS: (things to do, reminders, thoughts, etc.):

_____
_____
_____
_____
_____
_____
_____
_____
_____
_____
_____
_____

9 Understand the Power of Prayer, Meditation and Visualization

"The function of prayer is not to influence God, but rather to change the nature of the one who prays."
—Soren Kierkegaard

I pray daily. My prayers include what I want to happen in my life but also a great amount of gratitude for all the good that has occurred in my life and for the many gifts that have been bestowed upon me and my family. We all have been given unique gifts but many of us keep them to ourselves and feel afraid to share them with the world. A lot of people miss out on things when you don't share yourself that would greatly enrich your family, your community or the world. Don't let your fears and insecurities get in the way. Imagine if Shakespeare had never shared his plays or Oprah had been too afraid of speaking to a live studio audience to launch her own show.

It reminds me of the following bible story:

Jesus spoke a parable about a nobleman who gave his servants money to trade and invest until he returned from another country. When he returned one servant had taken the pound he was given and gained 10 pounds. The nobleman was pleased and rewarded him greatly. Another servant turned his pound into 5 pounds. Again the nobleman was pleased and rewarded the servant. He came across another servant who gave him back his pound with the explanation that he was afraid to let the nobleman down and feared losing the money so he kept the pound in a napkin for safe keeping. This upset the nobleman greatly. He not only did not receive a profit, but he didn't receive bank interest on his money. He ordered that what this servant had been given be taken from him and given to the most successful servants.

"But I say to you, that to everyone that hath shall be given, and he shall abound: and from him that hath not, even that which he hath, shall be taken from him." (St. Luke Chapter 20, verse 26)

Our talents and all those gifts from God are like the pound given to each servant. When we take our talents and divine gifts and share them with the world and use them to make things better we are like the successful servants. When we keep our talents to ourselves because we are too afraid to share with the world, too afraid to let someone down, too afraid of screwing up, we are like the servant who puts his pound in the napkin. And like that servant who had his gift given taken away, we too are losing or wasting our divine gifts if we don't use them and share them with others.

In my prayers I ask for divine assistance in using my gifts to the best of my abilities and to their highest potential. I ask for guidance, focus, strength and perseverance to accomplish my goals and that those goals be aligned with my divine purpose. I meditate on these things and on my affirmations while I practice deep and peaceful breathing. Finally, I take some time to allow my mind the freedom and fun to dream and visualize myself accomplishing those things I have outlined in my goals. I try to visualize myself in very vivid details. The more detail, the more real it is for me.

To give you an example how real my visualizations are for me I will share this story. I was standing in Wal-Mart looking at the bestselling books on the shelves and I saw my book on the shelf. I really felt my success and began to get very teary eyed. I've created a vision board where

Understand the Power of Prayer, Meditation and Visualization

I pasted pictures of those key things I want in my life along with key words expressing things I want to accomplish, qualities I want to develop and words and phrases that inspire me. Creating a vision board should be a really fun and exciting project and one that is great to do with kids too.

A few of the things on my board are:
- picture of the deck I want built on my house
- quote from Mahatma Gandhi: "You must be the change you wish to see in the world"
- phrase: Bestselling Author
- picture of the SUV and a beach house I want to own
- the words: LOVE, FAMILY, PRAYER, HEALTH, HAPPINESS, PROSPEROUS

You get the idea. Do everything you can to get vividly clear about what it is that you want in all areas of your life and what it really looks like for you. You can think about different areas of your life like Career, Health, Relationships, Family, Hobbies, and Spirituality.

In one of Mike Litman's talks he said, "You can only pursue what you see." In the book, Education of a Body Builder, Arnold Schwarzenegger discusses how he grew up with an image of his idol and studied him. He became obsessed with a picture of himself, what he wanted to become and eventually he did become just that. He won Mr. Universe at the age of 20 and went on to win the title of Mr. Olympia seven times. We can only attract what we see. Where's your inner vision taking you? What do you see? You can't outperform the picture. Without a vision, my dreams perish or never come to be. If you don't see what you want, you are not going to drum up the level of desire you need to obtain your goals. You must create a clear and definite picture of your future. Emmy winners often say, "I have been dreaming of this moment all my life."

The clearer you are about what you want, the clearer the action steps you need to take will become.

"Prayer is not asking. Prayer is putting oneself in the hands of God, at his disposition, and listening to His voice in the depth of our hearts."

—Mother Teresa

"Dreaming is not enough. You have to go a step further and use your imagination to visualize, with intent! Forget everything you've ever been taught, and believe it will happen, just as you imagined it. That is the secret. That is the mystery of life."

—Christine Anderson

"See things as you would have them be instead of as they are."

—Robert Collier

KEY POINTS: (things to do, reminders, thoughts, etc.):

_____
_____
_____
_____
_____
_____
_____
_____
_____
_____
_____
_____
_____
_____

10 You Deserve This, So No More Excuses

"He that is good for making excuses
is seldom good for anything else."
—Benjamin Franklin

If you find yourself not moving forward with your goals like you planned, check in with yourself. You probably have a lot of good reasons why you aren't taking action on your goals. I know I did. My kids have so much school work and if I don't help them, it won't get done. I'm sick. I mean I've been really sick, Mono, Lyme disease, kidney infections, thyroid problems, food allergies, adrenal issues and chronic fatigue. My job is very stressful and there are a lot of things there that require me to put in extra time. There are things I need to do at the house and work that I have to get done. The list goes on and on and my goals list also went on and on too because I wasn't achieving much on it. I felt like everyone else's needs were a priority over mine. I had to take care of everything for my kids, my husband and my job etc. All of their to do's and their needs came first. The worst part about it was I continuously felt inadequate because despite doing a whole lot of things for a whole lot of people I wasn't putting a dent in my goal list.

My goal list contained those things essential to me and my inner being. They are the things that make me feel alive and full of passion and excitement. If your goal list is the same, think about what I just said. The items that make me (you) feel alive and full of excitement. So if you aren't doing things on that list you're going to suffer because you're not giving yourself what you need to be completely happy. And most importantly, if you are not filled with excitement and joy for your life then everyone around you suffers too. Other people might not notice but they are not getting to experience the best version of you. I bet you never thought of it that way as you put everyone else first. It's important to find balance in everything you do.

I have mentioned some really good excuses and I'm sure you have some too. But the biggest eye opener for me was when I realized that even though I had some major things going on and some pretty significant illnesses, I was adequately accomplishing everything in my life except my personal goals, the things I wanted to do for me. Somehow everything else got prioritized and done whether I was sick or not and despite any other challenges. After doing some reflection, I noticed a pattern. Every time I started to do something for me that required me to move out of my comfort zone closer to achieving my goals, something always came up. One of my boys got sick. I got sicker or the kids had a string of projects. Work got crazy. Whatever it was, it always required my time and energy so much so that I had none left to work on my project. Remember in this scenario leaving my project until last is like filling up the jar with little rocks, sand and water and then trying to fit the big rocks in last. While it was happening, I felt a terrible tugging between what I felt I had to do and what I really wanted to do. I always chose what I felt I had to do and sometimes my challenges didn't let up until I stopped or gave up on what I wanted to do, my goal.

As I was reflecting upon my life over a period of a few years, I began to question how was it possible that every time I tried moving forward with certain goals things would go awry? I began to ask myself some serious questions and if you're not taking action to achieve your goals you should too. Were all the things I felt I had to do really necessary? Could I have asked someone else to help me out? What would have happened if I didn't do all the things I "felt" I had to do to be the perfect mother? Maybe my husband wouldn't do things the same as me but could he have completed the task? Was there someone at work I could have delegated things to rather than staying late every day?

Why am I not prioritizing what is necessary to achieve my goals? Am I afraid of failing or am I more afraid of succeeding? Is there some part of me deep down that doesn't feel I deserve to have the rewards that reaching my goals will bring? Am I afraid of the commitments I will have if I succeed? Am I afraid of not being good enough? What is it that is holding me back? I thought to myself as I realized it just doesn't seem possible for things to go wrong with perfect timing as they had over the years. As crazy as this may sound I felt that I had to be manifesting at least some of my own hardships. Whether it was an exacerbation of my sickness, children's activities, projects at work etc., these things were my excuses to not move forward, to stop taking action. Waiting to take the action steps towards our goals until EVERYTHING else is taken care is not a good plan because we often run out of time or energy before we get to them.

As I mentioned, there are some challenging things going on in my life and I have some really, really good excuses for not accomplishing my goals. However, one day I had an epiphany. It was like fumbling around in a dark room looking for something with no luck and someone turns on the light. Now I could see everything. Everything that I was doing now made sense. It wasn't good but now I was aware. Remember becoming aware of the issue is the first step to resolving it. I had these great excuses, why I hadn't done this or that and the truth was no one cared. Everyone is living their life, achieving their goals or not but certainly no one is concerned with my great excuses for not achieving my goals. No one but me cared about the excuses so who was I making up the excuses for and why did I need them? While my excuses kept me safe in my mind, they did nothing for my longing to achieve the goals that were near to my heart.

To break this pattern, I need to make sure I feel deserving of the rewards that come with achieving my goals. I do this by loving and appreciating myself and my own gifts. The gifts I have been blessed with that are meant to be shared with the world. I give myself the space I need and allow myself to say no to others sometimes for the sake of achieving my goals. I am important and the things I want for myself are important for me and more importantly for the whole world. When I am my true self and sharing my gifts with the world, everyone is better off. I use affirmations and self-talk to build myself up even when I don't believe it. I forgive myself for times when I feel I let myself down. I try to see myself like the little child who really wants to jump off the high dive to feel the amazing rush and sense of accomplishment once they do. That little child needs words of encouragement to take that last step off the dive so they don't turn around and go back down the stairs.

I made up my mind to be like the swim instructor who stood behind me as a little girl saying words of encouragement and not letting me go anywhere but off the dive. I decided to not accept excuses from myself anymore. No matter what the excuse is when I set the goals or the deadlines now and I become sick or something else goes awry, I tell myself that doesn't matter. Take the actions, meet the deadline, whatever it might be despite what is going on. Maybe it means that I don't do something as elaborately as I planned or I have to modify my original idea, but regardless I hold myself accountable and take the action. There are amazing stories everywhere we turn of people who overcame tremendous odds or incredible hurdles to accomplish great things. There is no reason why challenges and hurdles have to prevent me from achieving my goals. As I deny the excuses and make them irrelevant to taking my required actions, I've noticed that they have lessened and I believe will eventually go away altogether. There is a part of me that believes that the fatigue and sicknesses I have dealt with have been an excuse. With an excuse, I didn't have to really try to accomplish much. Sickness and fatigue have been a permanent excuse over the years to not take action and therefore neither fail nor succeed but to stay safe in my mind. What is your excuse? What keeps cropping up in your life that you are using as an excuse? I keep acknowledging to myself that I deserve happiness and that it's OK to try and fail or even to try and succeed. As long as you are trying to be the best version of you nothing else matters. The only way that you can be the best version of you is to keep digging deeper, taking action and putting yourself out there. And no matter what, I will not accept any more excuses from myself and you shouldn't either.

∎

"I attribute my success to this – I never gave or took any excuse."
—*Florence Nightingale*

"It is easier to move from failure to success than from excuses to success."
—*John C. Maxwell*

KEY POINTS: (things to do, reminders, thoughts, etc.):

_____
_____
_____
_____
_____
_____
_____
_____
_____
_____
_____
_____
_____
_____
_____
_____
_____

NOTES:

11
Thoughts for Getting Unstuck

"Any action is often better than no action, especially if you have been stuck in an unhappy situation for a long time. If it is a mistake, at least you learn something, in which case it's no longer a mistake. If you remain stuck, you learn nothing."

–*Eckhart Tolle*

If you are still not taking action, you may need to take some additional steps to get "Unstuck". When I'm in a rut it is often because I am not in the best place mentally or emotionally. To get into a better state of mind, there are a number of things I might do. Find something fun to do by myself or with friends/family or both. Anything that makes you laugh will increase your intake of oxygen-rich air and consequently, the endorphins released by your brain. This in turn can relieve stress as well as improve your mood. Spending time with good friends or family can also help you feel loved and supported which will help improve your mood.

I also will do some self-care. Get a massage, take a hot bath, a day of shopping, take a yoga class, or whatever self-care I am in need of. Revisiting all the things I am grateful for can also do wonders for my emotional state. I fill myself up with inspiration and try to surround myself with positive, motivating, healing words. Some inexpensive ways I boost my mental and emotional health are reading books, listening to CD's or watching DVDs and positive TV shows like those found on the Oprah network. It doesn't take long for me to feel inspired and motivated again.

Find motivational stories of people who overcame big challenges to make amazing contributions to the world. The internet is one great way to find these stories. I watched a video on YouTube recently about a man born with Cerebral Palsy. He could not speak well or control his hands and arms enough to write or do much else, but with a lot of patience, he could use 10 keys on a typewriter. Based on his disabilities, no one would have expected him to accomplish much, especially nothing meaningful in this world. Instead, he listened to a calling inside his body, a body that most of us would call broken. Using an old fashion typewriter and those 10 keys, he created the most amazing pictures. His artwork was as good as any artist.

I also watched another video on YouTube of an unbelievably inspiring man, a farmer. What could be so inspiring about the life of a farmer you ask? Well, this farmer didn't have any arms or legs but yet he drove large farm equipment, bailed hay and so on. He didn't focus on his limitations or what he couldn't do. Instead he focused on what he could do. And most importantly, he transcended social ideals of what he could do. Given the same situation handled differently, he could have easily been placed in an institution to be cared for. Instead he lives a productive life serving as a divine inspiration to us all. There are people all over the world who have overcome great odds to do amazing things by focusing on their talents rather than their disabilities. If you're stuck, find some of those stories and read/watch them. You might be so inspired that your hurdles shrink or disappear altogether.

One other tip that has helped me when I have felt stuck is thinking about success differently. Being a recovering perfectionist, I used to do a lot of judging and comparing and striving to be the best. I was recently working on a project and grooving right along when all of a sudden I noticed things weren't moving forward anymore. When I examined why,

I realized that I had reverted back to my old thinking. What if my work wasn't good enough? What if people didn't like it? I caught myself taking so much time debating over little things trying to make it "perfect." Thankfully, I recognized my old habits and did some reflection. I realized that I needed to think differently about my project and what I wanted to accomplish. I was thinking about my project in a way that could paralyze me. I was doing the project to put out to the world to judge, to decide if it's good enough, to decide if I get to succeed. Instead I realized it's something I need to do as an expression of me. If I take this action(s) to complete this "project" as a deeper expression of who I am and continue to take action to share more of my authentic self with the world, how can I fail? More importantly how can I not take the action?

If I think about my end goal of happiness which should be everyone's end goal, how can I be truly happy if I am not myself? If you are not in touch with who your true self is, then I suggest spending more time in prayer and meditation to get closer to God or whatever you feel the source of your being is. As you get closer to the source you will connect with your inner being. Use that connection to take steps towards becoming your most authentic self and then steps to start sharing that self with the rest of the world. There is not right or wrong, success or failure when you are expressing who you are because nobody can be YOU like YOU!! So stop thinking about everything you are trying to do in terms of what everyone else will think. Your action steps are really about YOU, so get busy and let yourself out to the rest of the world.

■

"It is common sense to take a method and try it. If it fails, admit it frankly and try another. But, above all, try something."

—*Franklin D. Roosevelt*

"The only thing that stands between a person and what they want is the will to try it and the faith to believe it is possible."

—*Rich DeVos*

Get Out of Your Head and Into Your Life!

"Surround yourself with people who lift you higher."

—*Oprah Winfrey*

KEY POINTS: (things to do, reminders, thoughts, etc.):

_____
_____
_____
_____
_____
_____
_____
_____
_____
_____
_____
_____
_____
_____
_____
_____
_____
_____

12 | Live in the Flow and Experience Synchronicity

"We do not create our destiny; we participate in its unfolding. Synchronicity works as a catalyst toward the working out of that destiny."
–David Richo

At one point I felt like I was really trying very hard and things just were not happening for me. I was thinking of people I wanted to talk to and going out of my way to search them out but nothing was happening. I was becoming frustrated and worn out. It felt like I did not have enough hours in the day (a good time to put some affirmations into place☺). I thought to myself, who do I know? What is close to me?

It shouldn't seem so hard. Then I started to pay attention to what was happening around me instead of fixating on the specific path I created in my goal setting.

Please do not misunderstand. I am not saying don't pay attention to your goals, but what I am saying is pay attention to the opportunities that come your way. Be open to them even if they don't seem to fit neatly with your goals. Look for the synchronicity in your life. With synchronicity, forces greater than us are at work. While we might have goals and a path to obtain those goals written out, God, or Divine wisdom may show us a different path. By paying attention to synchronicity, these opportunities will present themselves to you with ease. They may even lead you to your ultimate goal or to something bigger and better. They may lead you down a different path that will ultimately get you to the same destination; one you may never reach if you are fixated on going down one path and one path only.

For example, let's say I wanted to speak about nutrition at my local school but despite my phone calls, I don't get through. Meanwhile, I happen to sit with the director of the YMCA at a local benefit who talks with me and is very interested in bringing in a nutrition speaker. My first goal was not giving talks at the YMCA, but the opportunity easily presented itself and it fits in my schedule and it is not antagonistic to my overall vision and goal. So instead of turning it down, I consider synchronicity and stay open to all possibilities. I begin talks at the YMCA. As it turns out, a very dear friend of the school superintendent often attends talks at the YMCA and attends one of mine. She loves it and thinks I should talk at the local schools. She calls her friend, the superintendent, to arrange a meeting for me.

Don't get so fixated on getting in through the locked front door that you forget to check the back door or even the first floor windows. If things are coming to you with ease and there is synchronicity in it, pay attention and things may just fall into place. Be clear on your vision and goals but stay open to all possibilities related to how you might achieve them. Be aware of the synchronistic possibilities because they are not always what you are looking for. Sometimes they are subtle and if you are not paying attention you will miss them. I want to be clear that I am not discounting focus and persistence. I just want you to be open to different paths and different action steps for accomplishing what you want.

Life will not take us where we want to go if we are not ready. But how do you get ready? Mike Litman says, "You don't have to get it right, you just have to get it going."

Just keep doing! Keep improving yourself and taking action. Sooner or later you will get where you want to be. It's kind of like taking a trip with some road construction. If you turned back or quit every time you hit a detour, you'd never get to your final destination. Instead just take the detours with faith, one instruction at a time and know it might take you a little longer or a different way than you had originally planned but you will get to your destination. You may even discover something greater and more fulfilling along the way.

Have you ever had something go wrong and ended up having the most incredible experience or met a wonderful person that would never have been possible if things had gone exactly according to plan? When you hit detours in the road, you don't usually question that you will get to your final destination. So don't question it when you run across them in life. Just keep moving forward and trust that like your trip you will get there. Most importantly try to enjoy the ride. Life is about enjoying the journey. While you will achieve milestones along the way, if they are your only enjoyment, you are missing out on having fun in your life.

To summarize, once I gained momentum from my new and good, I began focusing my thoughts on taking action. I got clear on what actions I wanted to take by getting clear on my goals and focusing on them. I aligned my thoughts and beliefs with my goals. I prayed about it and saw myself achieving them with affirmations, visualization and synchronicity.

Once I began aligning everything I could with my desired outcomes—my goals, my thoughts, my beliefs, my actions—things just started happening. People and events started popping up and moving me more toward the goals I wanted to achieve. Sometimes I had to take a step back to see what I was gaining from the experience but almost always I could see how it related. I'm still working on doing things consistently and find myself backsliding into some of my old habits and routines if I am not careful. Consequently, I continue to focus on consistently taking action and creating lifelong habits.

"According to Vedanta, there are only two symptoms of enlightenment, just two indications that a transformation is taking place within you toward a higher consciousness. The first symptom is that you stop worrying. Things don't bother you anymore. You become light-hearted and full of joy. The second symptom is that you encounter more and more meaningful coincidences in your life, more and more synchronicities. And this accelerates to the point where you actually experience the miraculous." (quoted by Carol Lynn Pearson in Consider the Butterfly)

–Deepak Chopra

"I am open to the guidance of synchronicity, and do not let expectations hinder my path."

–Dali Lama

KEY POINTS: (things to do, reminders, thoughts, etc.):

13
Develop Consistent Habits

"Motivation will help you begin your journey,
but your habits will determine your destination."

–Unknown

Creating consistent habits is where so many of us fall short in life. We do all the right things many times over but we don't do them consistently. I cannot stress enough that you have to develop habits of success. If you talk to any successful person, they will describe consistent habits and routines. Many books have been written on this topic and one of my favorites is "The 7 Habits of Highly Effective People," by Stephen R. Covey. When he speaks about the 7 habits overview, he says that habits are defined as the intersection of knowledge (what to do and why), skill (the how to do) and desire (the motivation, the want to do). He says, "In order to make something a habit in our lives, we have to have all three."

He also provides a quote from Aristotle, "We are what we repeatedly do. Excellence, then, is not an act, but a habit." Wow! Powerful stuff!

If you examine your own life, are there areas you want to improve? I bet if you look at any one of the areas, you will find that there are actions you know you should be taking but you are not doing them consistently. Take some time to examine your life and what you were doing at times when you felt that you had good momentum and things were going well. Figure out what you were doing. Write it down and make it a goal to do those things consistently. Creating habits and doing all the things I talked about in this book and any others that you identify for yourself consistently without fail will be the difference between existing in an average state and propelling yourself into a state of excellence.

How many people eat healthy for a week or two and then return to their old ways before ever reaping the benefits? If they would stick to the healthy eating through the uncomfortable period, they would get to the place of excellence—the place where they are enjoying better health, more energy and many other benefits. Most of us forget that we have to bear some discomfort as we adjust to new routines in order to gain the benefits. Worse yet, we do this to ourselves over and over. We start something, experience the discomfort for a while and give up. Then because we know we should be doing it, we begin the process all over again at some point. We do this over and over and experience the discomfort over and over. Wouldn't it be much easier to stick it out a little longer the first time than to torture yourself? Don't give up so soon. Think about how much more discomfort you will have by quitting and beginning again and again. Start taking steps today to set up systems in your planner that create habits and make you take consistent action. Taking action is good, but it is in taking consistent action that the greater rewards come.

In closing, just be you. You are a unique and special gift from God. When we all are doing what we were created to do, our planet exists in harmony. When we make ourselves be people we are not, God's plan is out of balance and the world is not in harmony. Explore who you really are. Develop goals that allow you to express who you really are and take action, to achieve those goals. Allow yourself to experience your inner passions and let your life flow from them. Take the steps we talked about. Short and sweet, pray to get clear on your divine purpose and what you want to do. Create goals and take consistent action.

Use the tools I have outlined and the notes that you have taken to help you stay motivated and on track. Only pay attention to the thoughts that are serving you. Most of all, know that life is long and fluid. It's constantly changing and so are you. Remember life is not just about reaching goals and arriving at destinations. Life is about enjoying the process and the journey. Create lots of good memories. Have lots of fun. Make many friends. Help lots of people. Enjoy nature. Don't just let life happen. Get out of your head and into your life. Start creating the life you want and take action today to make it happen.

∎

"Your beliefs become your thoughts,

Your thoughts become your words,

Your words become your actions,

Your actions become your habits,

Your habits become your values,

Your values become your destiny."

–Mahatma Gandhi

"We are what we repeatedly do. Excellence then, is not an act, but a habit."

–Aristotle

Get Out of Your Head and Into Your Life!

KEY POINTS: (things to do, reminders, thoughts, etc.):

About the Author

Kim has worked in the healthcare management field for 25 years. In her most recent role, she serves as the Director of Medical Information Services which supports the electronic health record in large number of company owned physician offices. She is a dedicated mother and wife. She and her husband of more than 15 years are blessed with two talented boys that they enjoy coaching and watching play sports. Kim is also a Certified Holistic Health Counselor, Certified in Lifestyle Medicine, an accomplished athlete, recently inducted into the Mercer County Hall of Fame and a coach of various sports.

She is passionate about writing, sports and holistic health.

She believes words can change the world and plans to use her talents as a writer to make it a better place one book at time.

For more information about Kim or her services email:
kimladjevich@yahoo.com

OR visit: *kim-ladjevich.healthcoach.integrativenutrition.com*

www.ingramcontent.com/pod-product-compliance
Lightning Source LLC
Chambersburg PA
CBHW071324040426
42444CB00009B/2078